Shaun the Sheep™

You Are My Mum!

Series Director: Richard (Golly) Goleszowski
Adapted by Monica Hughes

Shaun was looking at some eggs.

Crack!

Chicks came out of the eggs.

The chicks ran to Shaun.
Shaun did not want to look after them.

Mum!

He put the chicks in a bucket ...

... but they got out!
Shaun was not happy.

He put the chicks in the shed ...

... but they got out!
Shaun was not happy.

The hen did not see the chicks.

The hen went to look for the chicks.
She was not happy.

Shaun got the chicks for the hen.

The chicks did not want the hen.
The chicks wanted Shaun.

The hen was not happy.

Shaun was not happy.

Then Shaun had a plan!

14

Now the hen was soft like Shaun. The hen was happy. The chicks were happy too.

But Shaun was not happy.
Shaun was cold!